NFL
TODAY

THE STORY OF THE
PHILADELPHIA EAGLES

THE STORY OF THE PHILADELPHIA EAGLES

TYLER OMOTH

CREATIVE EDUCATION

Cover: Eagles defense, 1962 (top), safety Brian
Dawkins (bottom)
Page 2: 2005 Philadelphia Eagles
Pages 4–5: Linebacker Chuck Bednarik (right)
Pages 6–7: Cornerback Asante Samuel

Published by Creative Education
P.O. Box 227, Mankato, Minnesota 56002
Creative Education is an imprint of
The Creative Company
www.thecreativecompany.us

Design and production by Blue Design
Design Associate: Sarah Yakawonis
Printed by Corporate Graphics
in the United States of America

Photographs by AP Images, Corbis (Bettmann,
Richard Cummins), Getty Images (Vernon Biever/NFL
Photos, Jerry Driendl, Stephen Dunn, Chris Gardner,
Drew Hallowell, Harry How, Kidwiler Collection/
Diamond Images, Harold M. Lambert/Lambert,
Kirby Lee/NFL, Hunter Martin, Hunter Martin/NFL,
Al Messerschmidt, Ronald C. Modra/Sports Imagery,
NFL, Doug Pensinger, Robert Riger, Eliot J. Schechter,
Jamie Squire, Vic Stein/NFL, Thomas E. Witte)

Library of Congress Cataloging-in-Publication Data

Omoth, Tyler.
The story of the Philadelphia Eagles / by Tyler
Omoth.
p. cm. — (NFL today)
Includes index.
ISBN 978-1-58341-766-9
1. Philadelphia Eagles (Football team)—History—
Juvenile literature. I. Title. II. Series.

GV956.P44O66 2009
796.332'640974811—dc22   2008022697

CPSIA: 020212 PO1534
9 8 7 6 5 4 3

CONTENTS

X

X

ON THE SIDELINES

MEET THE EAGLES

THE EAGLES TAKE FLIGHT

X- -

X The sixth-most populous city in the United States, Philadelphia is rich in both American history and sports tradition, boasting big-league franchises in all of the four major sports.

In the late 1700s, as the United States was establishing its independence from England, few cities played as important a part as Philadelphia, Pennsylvania. The Declaration of Independence and the Constitution were both signed in Philadelphia. The city even served as America's capital from 1790 to 1800. When the American people were fighting for freedom, Philadelphia was a center for both military and diplomatic strategy.

It is fitting, therefore, that the city is home to a professional football team called the Eagles, as the eagle is a classic symbol of American freedom. The city's team did not start out as the Eagles, however. It didn't even start out in Philadelphia. The franchise originated in Frankford, Pennsylvania, in 1924 as the Yellow Jackets. It wasn't until 1933 that former University of Pennsylvania teammates Bert Bell and Lud Wray purchased the National Football League (NFL) team and brought the newly named Eagles to Philadelphia.

Despite the heroics of tiny quarterback Davey O'Brien and tough-as-nails end Bill Hewitt (who refused to wear a helmet until the league made it mandatory in 1939), the Eagles never finished higher than third in the NFL's five-team Eastern Division in the 1930s. In 1935, Bell proposed that the NFL begin an annual draft for college players to fairly distribute

talent throughout the league. The idea took root, and Philadelphia received the very first pick in the inaugural 1936 draft, choosing University of Chicago halfback Jay Berwanger, who had won the Heisman Trophy as college football's best player. Unfortunately, the pick backfired on the Eagles when Berwanger announced that he had no intentions of playing pro ball and never signed with the team.

The Eagles were sold in 1941 to wealthy steel businessman Alexis Thompson, who immediately hired Earle "Greasy" Neale as the club's coach. Neale had proven his ability as a longtime coach in the college ranks and even led Washington & Jefferson College to the 1922 Rose Bowl. With Neale's hiring, the first part of Philadelphia's championship formula was in place.

As young men went overseas to fight in World War II in the early '40s, the NFL struggled with a shortage of players. To field a team, the Eagles formed a temporary merger with the Pittsburgh Steelers in 1943. The "Steagles" proved to be a formidable team, posting a 5–4–1 record, the first winning season for Philadelphia. But after just one season, the Phil-Pitt merger was dissolved, and Philadelphia had its own team back.

In 1944, the Eagles drafted the second part of their championship formula: running back Steve Van Buren. Playing alongside quarterback Tommy Thompson and (starting in 1947) two-way end Pete Pihos, Van Buren quickly gave

EARLE "GREASY" NEALE

COACH
EAGLES SEASONS: 1941-50

If a team is only as good as the man leading it, then Earle "Greasy" Neale—who kept his team at the top of its game for nearly a decade—is surely one of the best coaches in Eagles history. Neale (pictured, center) led the Eagles to three straight Eastern Division crowns from 1947 to 1949 and two NFL championships in 1948 and 1949. The back-to-back championships were won in shutouts, a feat that still has not been duplicated by any other team. Neale loved to study game film, and his observations helped him produce many innovative ideas that remain a part of the game today. Neale's most important innovation, however, was the "Eagle Defense," which later evolved into the "4-3" defense (four linemen and three linebackers) that is still common in today's game. Before he earned renown as a football coach, Neale earned a measure of success in professional baseball as a young man. He played outfield for the Cincinnati Reds and hit for a .357 average during the 1919 World Series

FOOTBALL ON THE SMALL SCREEN

Professional football has enjoyed remarkable popularity among the American public, a fact that can be largely attributed to its relationship with television. Fast-paced and exciting, the NFL's high level of football is perfect for the small screen, and it all started on October 22, 1939, when the Philadelphia Eagles played in the very first televised NFL game. In front of 13,050 fans at Ebbets Field in New York, the Eagles matched up against Brooklyn's Dodgers and their star quarterback, Ace Parker. The NBC network broadcast the game to approximately 500 television sets in the New York area, as well as a special viewing of the game at the site of New York's World's Fair. The broadcast didn't have any commercials to interrupt the action, but the early broadcast equipment periodically lost picture due to cloud cover that blocked out the light that the cameras needed. When the screen would go blank, the broadcast team would simply revert to a radio broadcast until the clouds passed and there was adequate light again. The Eagles lost the game 23–14 but earned a special place in NFL broadcasting history.

Philadelphia one of the most feared offenses in the league. The Eagles soared up the standings, finishing 1944 with a 7–1–2 record.

In 1947, Philadelphia finally claimed its first Eastern Division title. The Eagles fell a touchdown short to the Chicago Cardinals in the 1947 NFL Championship Game, but they came back in 1948 hungrier than ever. After going 9–2–1, the Eagles found themselves in a rematch with Chicago for the NFL title. On an almost unplayable, snow-covered field in Philadelphia's Shibe Park, the game went scoreless until

X Drafted in 1945 but unable to enter the NFL until 1947 due to military service, sure-handed and powerful end Pete Pihos (number 35) starred in Philadelphia for nine seasons.

the fourth quarter, when Van Buren powered into the end zone for the game's only touchdown and the Eagles' first NFL championship.

The next season, Coach Neale led the Eagles to an 11–1 mark and a return to the NFL Championship Game. Playing this time on the mud-soaked field of the Los Angeles Memorial Coliseum, Van Buren set an NFL playoff record with 196 rushing yards as the Eagles blanked the Los Angeles Rams 14–0. Van Buren was the hero again, but the Eagles players gave much of the credit to Neale. "Most of the success of the Eagles must go to Greasy Neale," Eagles linebacker and center Alex Wojciechowicz later said. "Of my 13 years in the league, there were none greater. He was a fine teacher and leader."

The heart of the Philadelphia teams of the '50s was Chuck Bednarik. After being drafted by the Eagles in 1949, the former University of Pennsylvania All-American made an immediate impact, starting at linebacker on Philadelphia's 1949 championship team. The Eagles quickly realized that Bednarik was too valuable to waste on the sidelines and made him—like Wojciechowicz before him—the starting center as well. So rarely did Bednarik come out of games that he became known as the "60-Minute Man." Playing through torn

STEVE VAN BUREN

RUNNING BACK
EAGLES SEASONS: 1944-51
HEIGHT: 6 FEET
WEIGHT: 200 POUNDS

Before the Eagles selected Steve Van Buren with the fifth overall pick in the 1944 NFL Draft, the team had never finished above fourth place in its division. Van Buren immediately took his place as one of the best athletes in the NFL and soon led Philadelphia to three consecutive division titles and two NFL championships. In 1945, Van Buren earned a remarkable "triple crown" by leading the league in rushing yards, points scored, and kickoff return yards. He excelled by using a relentless running style that wore down opposing defenses and created running holes where there were none. One of his most memorable performances came in the 1949 NFL Championship Game, when he carried the ball 31 times for 196 yards in the Eagles' 14–0 victory over the Los Angeles Rams. "They were the glamour boys of the NFL. They were a great team," Eagles linebacker and center Chuck Bednarik said of the Rams. "But he just put us on his shoulders and absolutely ran wild on that day." When Van Buren retired in 1951, he was the NFL's all-time leading rusher with a total of 5,860 yards.

The 1948 NFL Championship Game was so snowy that fans were admitted for free if they helped shovel off the field.

tendons and broken bones, Bednarik would miss only 3 games in 14 NFL seasons.

Although the Eagles did not excel as a team for much of the 1950s, they did treat fans to some impressive individual performances. In 1953, quarterbacks Bobby Thomason and Adrian Burk combined to pass for a league-high 3,250 yards, while Pihos led the league with 1,049 receiving yards and 10 touchdowns. The next year, wide receiver and placekicker Bobby Walston topped the league in scoring with 114 points.

In 1958, the team moved from Shibe Park (which had been renamed Connie Mack Stadium in 1953) to the larger University of Pennsylvania's Franklin Field, enabling their fan attendance to nearly double. That year, Bednarik suffered a knee injury that robbed him of the mobility needed to play linebacker. Yet he inspired talented teammates such as running back Tommy McDonald and receiver Pete Retzlaff by continuing to snap the ball on offense. It was this type of toughness that helped keep the team respectable during the playoff drought of the '50s.

SOARING TO
ANOTHER
CHAMPIONSHIP

X - - - - - - - - - - - - - -

In 1958, Philadelphia brought in another player who would

eventually be enshrined in the Pro Football Hall of Fame:

former Los Angeles Rams quarterback Norm "The Dutchman"

Van Brocklin. Although the Eagles had to trade two starting

players and a draft pick to the Rams to get the quarterback,

no one in Philadelphia complained. Van Brocklin's on-field

leadership and great passing arm carried the Eagles to an

improved 7–5 mark in 1959.

In 1960, the Eagles peaked. After losing two lineback-

ers to injuries late in the season, Philadelphia reinstated

Bednarik's 60-minute workload. The Eagles and their vet-

eran iron man rolled to a 10–2 record and won the Eastern

Conference title. Philadelphia then faced off against leg-

endary coach Vince Lombardi and the Green Bay Packers in

the NFL Championship Game.

The game was a hard-fought contest between two of

the toughest teams in football. The Eagles trailed 13–10 in

the fourth quarter before The Dutchman—as he had done

all season—engineered a game-winning drive. "He was like a

coach on the field," Bednarik said of Van Brocklin, who was

named the NFL's Most Valuable Player (MVP) of the 1960 season.

Philadelphia fans savored the 1960 season, and it was a

good thing, because it would take 18 years and 6 different

CHAMPIONS AGAIN

Led by quarterback Norm Van Brocklin and "60-Minute Man" Chuck Bednarik, the 1960 Eagles fought their way to the NFL Championship Game for the third time in 13 seasons. The game was played at the Eagles' home venue, Franklin Field, against the Western Conference champion Green Bay Packers. After legendary quarterback Bart Starr and his fellow Packers took an early lead with 2 field goals, the Eagles put 10 points on the board before the half. After a scoreless third quarter, the Packers took a 13–10 lead early in the fourth quarter. Eagles running back Ted Dean then took matters into his own hands, returning the ensuing kickoff deep into Packers territory and shortly thereafter running the ball into the end zone to give Philadelphia the lead again. The Packers launched one last drive, but Bednarik stepped up to stop running back Jim Taylor on the Eagles' eight-yard line as the clock ran out. The champion Eagles had handed Packers coach Vince Lombardi his only career playoff loss. "The tackle I made on Taylor was the greatest play I ever made," Bednarik later said.

coaches before the Eagles made the playoffs again. Still, the team put on some good shows in the 1960s, including a remarkable 1961 season by new quarterback Sonny Jurgensen, who passed for 3,723 yards and 32 touchdowns. Fans also saw an NFL record-setting performance (2,306 all-purpose yards) by running back Timmy Brown in 1962. The next year, the Eagles were purchased by Washington, D.C., businessman Jerry Wolman who, despite numerous trades, could not field a winning team in Philadelphia.

The Eagles were sold again in 1969 to a millionaire trucking executive named Leonard Tose, who reportedly paid $16.1 million dollars for the Philadelphia franchise—a record price for the purchase of any professional sports team at the time. Two years later, he moved the team from Franklin Field to Veterans Stadium, which the Eagles would call home for the next three decades.

It was more of the same for the Eagles in the early 1970s, as the team consistently failed to assemble a winning season. In 1972, receiver Harold Jackson led the league in both receptions (62) and receiving yards (1,048). The next year, a towering young receiver named Harold Carmichael emerged to lead the league with 67 catches. Yet despite such strong performances, the Eagles were a team that just couldn't fly.

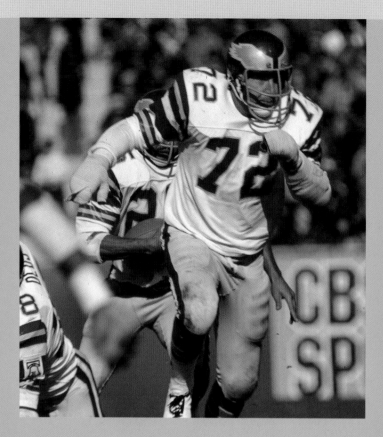

X Wade Key helped anchor the left side of Philadelphia's offensive line as both a guard and a tackle throughout the 1970s, helping the Eagles make the playoffs in 1978 and 1979.

Things finally changed for the better in 1976, when Dick Vermeil was named head coach. Vermeil believed that the only path to greatness was through hard work, and "Coach V" worked tirelessly to turn the Eagles around, often sleeping in his office instead of at home. "I don't want to put our other coaches down," Tose said as he introduced Vermeil. "But I'm telling you that this time the Philadelphia fans are getting the real thing—a great coach."

In 1978, Coach Vermeil's efforts paid off as the Eagles went 9–7 and returned to the playoffs for the first of two straight seasons. Although fans were disappointed when the team suffered playoff defeats both times, they were sure the Eagles could win it all if Coach Vermeil could get his team to improve one more notch.

Coach Dick Vermeil was renowned for his work ethic, while his quarterback, Ron Jaworski, was known for his durability, setting an NFL record by starting 116 straight games. **X**

CHUCK BEDNARIK

CENTER, LINEBACKER
EAGLES SEASONS: 1949-62
HEIGHT: 6-FOOT-3
WEIGHT: 233 POUNDS

Chuck Bednarik was a true iron man of the NFL. Playing center on offense and middle linebacker on defense, the hard-nosed star was even on the field for special-teams plays. On offense, he was a bulldozing blocker, and as a linebacker, he was a feared hitter. Bednarik is best known for two remarkable plays, both of which occurred during the 1960 season. The first happened in a game against the New York Giants. As New York tried to mount a fourth-quarter comeback in a 17–10 game, the "60-Minute Man" hit Giants star running back Frank Gifford hard enough to both cause a game-ending fumble and knock Gifford out cold. Then, late in the 1960 NFL Championship Game, with Philadelphia leading 17–13, Green Bay Packers halfback Jim Taylor was streaking toward the end zone before the 35-year-old Bednarik ran him down and wrestled him to the ground as the clock expired. During and after his football career, Bednarik also sold concrete, prompting a local sportswriter to dub him "Concrete Charlie," stating that he was "as hard as the concrete he sells."

Thanks to a strong offensive showing in 1980 by Carmichael, quarterback Ron Jaworski, and veteran running back Wilbert Montgomery, Philadelphia surged to the top of the National Football Conference's (NFC) East Division. "Philly" fans then cheered as the Eagles flew by the Minnesota Vikings and Dallas Cowboys to land in Super Bowl XV, where they faced the Oakland Raiders.

Although the Raiders topped the Eagles 27–10 on Super Bowl Sunday at the Louisiana Superdome, the Eagles held their heads high. "Four years ago, this team was a doormat," said Jaworski, who was named the NFL's Player of the Year. "Now we're Super Bowl material. You know how satisfying that is?"

Coach Vermeil led the Eagles back to the playoffs in 1981 but then resigned just nine victories short of surpassing Greasy Neale as the winningest coach in franchise history. In seven seasons, Coach V had guided the Eagles to 57 victories, 7 playoff games, 1 Super Bowl ... and newfound respectability.

THE HAPPY HUNDRED

Football fans love to feel like they're a part of their favorite team. In 1949, Eagles fans got that chance in a very real way as the team was sold to 100 buyers who each paid $3,000 for their share. The group included some of the most prominent names on the Philadelphia business and political scene and was nicknamed "The Happy Hundred" or "The 100 Brothers." The Happy Hundred could brag that they were part-owners of their favorite NFL team for parts of three decades and even won an NFL championship in 1960. This arrangement stayed in place for 13 years, although some of the investors had sold their shares to others within the original 100. By 1963, the remaining investors agreed to sell the team. The asking price for the shares was $4.5 million, but after a bidding war, the team was purchased by Jerry Wolman, a 36-year-old business executive from Washington, D.C., for $5.5 million. By 2008, the Green Bay Packers were the only American professional sports team that was still owned by public shareholders.

THE MINISTER AND THE SCRAMBLER

Without Coach Vermeil, the Eagles stumbled badly over the next several years. Philadelphia clearly needed something big, and in 1985, it got it in the form of 6-foot-5 and 300-pound defensive end Reggie White. White was an ordained Baptist minister who had earned the nickname "The Minister of Defense" while dominating the United States Football League as part of a team called the Memphis Showboats. Once signed by the Eagles, the enormous end made 13 quarterback sacks to earn 1985 NFL Defensive Rookie of the Year honors.

Unfortunately for Eagles opponents, that was just the beginning. Playing alongside defensive linemen Greg Brown and Ken Clarke, White spearheaded an increasingly frightening pass rush. In 1986, he added 18 sacks to Brown and Clarke's combined 17. By the time he ended his Philadelphia career in 1992, White would be the only

The Eagles defense grew into a hard-hitting force in the late '80s, with the line being led by end Reggie White (number 92), and the secondary being led by safety Andre Waters (left). **X**------

HAROLD CARMICHAEL

WIDE RECEIVER
EAGLES SEASONS: 1971-83
HEIGHT: 6-FOOT-8
WEIGHT: 225 POUNDS

A quarterback loves a big target. That's especially true when his team is in the red zone (inside the 20-yard line) and ready to score. Harold Carmichael was a full 6-foot-8 when he lined up for the Eagles. His size alone created matchup problems for defenses, who would try to double-team him with two cornerbacks that were frequently almost a foot shorter than he was. Eagles quarterbacks such as Ron Jaworski needed only to throw the ball up high, and Carmichael would go up and snatch it out of the air above the defenders' heads. But Carmichael was more than just a tall body. He was a fast runner with rare leaping ability and remarkable durability. Between 1972 and 1983, he played in 162 straight games for the Eagles. Carmichael appeared in four Pro Bowls and still holds Eagles franchise records for touchdowns (79), games played (180), receiving yards (8,978), and receptions (589). "He was the first big receiver in the NFL," said Alva Tabor, who coached Carmichael at Louisiana's Southern University and A&M College. "Harold actually changed the game."

player in NFL history to have more sacks (124) than games played (121).

Hoping to build a mighty defense around White, the Eagles hired former Chicago Bears defensive coordinator Buddy Ryan as head coach in 1986. Coach Ryan began installing the same defensive game plan that he had used to propel the 1985 Bears to a Super Bowl victory. And while he was thrilled with some of the team's defensive talent, Ryan was perhaps most impressed with young quarterback Randall Cunningham.

During his college career at the University of Nevada, Las Vegas, the tall and lanky Cunningham had proven to be a sensational athlete, able to sprint like a wide receiver or to

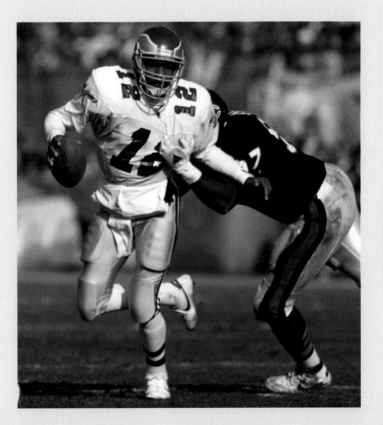

X Never reluctant to run with the ball, Randall Cunningham was among the most frequently sacked passers in the game, but he could also break loose for big gains on any given play.

REGGIE WHITE

DEFENSIVE END
EAGLES SEASONS: 1985–92
HEIGHT: 6-FOOT-5
WEIGHT: 300 POUNDS

Dubbed "The Minister of Defense" during his senior season at the University of Tennessee after becoming an ordained minister at age 17, White brought a rare passion for stopping opposing offenses with him to the NFL. He gave Eagles fans a glimpse of the future in 1985 as he tallied 2.5 sacks in his very first game and 13 sacks in only 13 games his first season, earning Defensive Rookie of the Year honors. Year after year, he put up double-digit sack totals, and he was selected to 13 straight Pro Bowls. In 1987, White put together one of the best years by any defensive lineman in history by collecting 21 sacks during a strike-shortened season that lasted just 12 games. Although White was dominant at disrupting offenses and harrying quarterbacks on the field, he was also considered a valuable leader and mentor to his teammates. After White passed away in 2006, former NFL commissioner Paul Tagliabue summarized his legacy by saying, "Reggie White was a gentle warrior who will be remembered as one of the greatest defensive players in NFL history."

launch the ball more than 70 yards down the field. Finally given the chance to start in 1987, Cunningham made good on the opportunity by throwing 23 touchdown passes. After the season, as Cunningham recalled, "Buddy came to me and said, 'It's your offense. If it doesn't work, it's going to be your fault.' I don't mind that at all."

Philadelphia fans didn't mind either, as Cunningham and the Eagles began to soar. In 1988, he and rookie tight end Keith Jackson led the team to a 10–6 record and a playoff berth. Unfortunately, the Eagles lost to the Bears 20–12 in a bizarre, mist-shrouded playoff game dubbed "The Fog Bowl." The next year, the defense notched a team-record 62 sacks as the Eagles stormed to an 11–5 mark and another playoff berth. But the strong offense of the Los Angeles Rams was too much for the Eagles, as Los Angeles dealt Philadelphia a 21–7 defeat.

In 1990, Cunningham enjoyed the best season of his Philadelphia career, throwing for 3,466 yards and running for an incredible 942 more. Unfortunately, despite his efforts and those of White, Jackson, and defensive tackle Jerome Brown, the Eagles lost in the first round of the playoffs for a third straight year. Coach Ryan was then fired, and White and Jackson soon left town. It was time for the Eagles to rebuild.

The 1996 season was the best of halfback Ricky Watters's career, as he carried the ball 353 times and gained 1,855 yards on runs and passes—tops in the NFL in both categories. **X**

The mid-1990s were mediocre seasons in Philadelphia. The Eagles made the postseason in 1995 with a 10–6 record under head coach Ray Rhodes and even blew out the Detroit Lions, 58–37, in a playoff game. But the eventual Super Bowl champion Dallas Cowboys crushed them a week later, 30–11. New standouts such as fiery running back Ricky Watters stepped forward, but they couldn't stop the downward slide. By 1998, the once-mighty Eagles were just 3–13.

FLY, EAGLES, FLY!

When Jerry Wolman owned the Eagles during the 1960s, his daughter frequently accompanied him to games. After hearing the rival Washington Redskins fans belt out their team's war chant, she implored her father to let her create a song that would rally Eagles fans and energize their stadium for home games. The resulting song was "Fly, Eagles, Fly!" The fight song was a hit with fans, but after a few years, its popularity waned. It wasn't until Jeffrey Lurie bought the Eagles in 1994 that the song was brought back to the stadium to be blasted through the stadium loudspeakers during Eagles games once again. Eagles fans latched on to the old song and today sing it after every touchdown and sometimes for no apparent reason at all. The song has even been heard at Philadelphia Phillies baseball, Flyers hockey, 76ers basketball, and Soul arena football games. Fans sometimes take liberties with the words to include their current opponent in the song. After more than four decades, "Fly, Eagles, Fly!" remains one of the most popular team anthems in the NFL.

REID TAKES
THE REINS

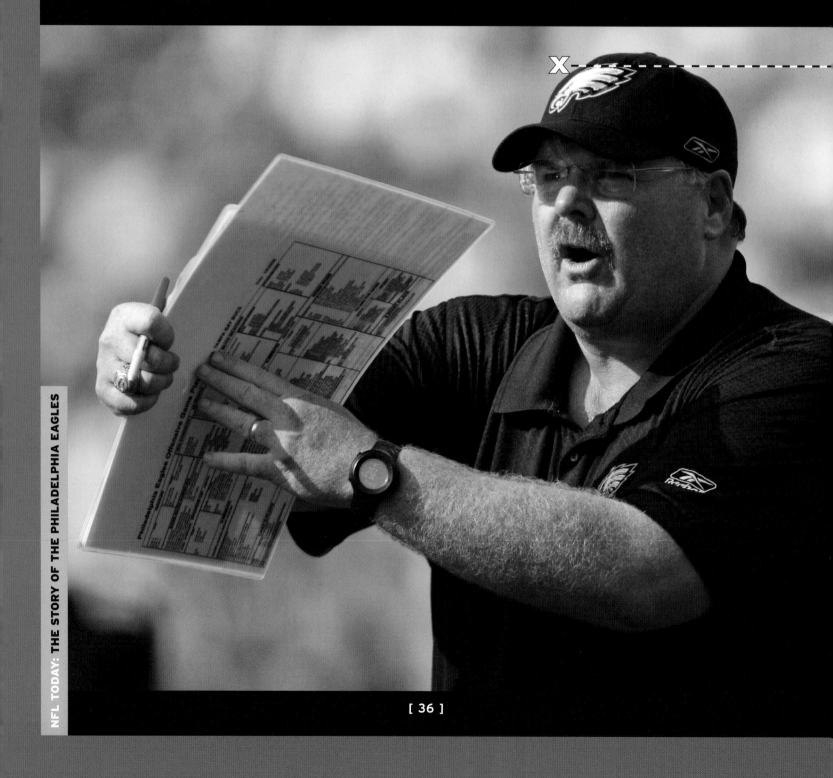

When former Green Bay Packers assistant coach Andy Reid
was named head coach in 1999, things began looking up in
Philly. The team went 5–11 in its first season under Reid. Then,
with linemen Hugh Douglas and Corey Simon leading a brawny
defense, the 2000 Eagles suddenly soared to the top of the
NFC East with an 11–5 record.

The biggest story in 2000 was that of quarterback
Donovan McNabb. In just his second NFL season, the
youngster earned comparisons to Randall Cunningham by
throwing for 3,365 yards and running for 629. He then led
the Eagles to a 21–3 playoff victory over the Tampa Bay
Buccaneers. "Donovan's a sharp kid," Coach Reid said, "and I
know he'll turn into a top-notch quarterback."

For the next two seasons, McNabb and the Eagles
advanced to the NFC Championship Game. Unfortunately,
they came up just one victory short of the Super Bowl both
times, losing to the St. Louis Rams in 2001 and the Buccaneers
in 2002. The 2002 defeat was particularly disappointing to

Philly fans, as it was the last game ever played in Veterans

Stadium, the team's home since 1971.

After moving into their new home, Lincoln Financial Field,

the Eagles lost their first two games of the 2003 season.

However, Philadelphia then rallied to an NFC-best 12–4 record.

The stout defense was bolstered by Brian Dawkins, one of

the game's hardest-hitting safeties. Running back Brian

Westbrook, meanwhile, led the team in rushing, was vital

as a receiver, and was dangerous as a return man on both

punts and kickoffs. "He's so good for us," said Eagles general

manager Tom Heckert, "because he's such a dynamic weapon.

If you talk to [defensive] coordinators, they think he's the

hardest guy to defend."

Philadelphia sneaked by Green Bay in a fiercely played

playoff game that culminated in a fourth-and-26 situation

for the Eagles. McNabb converted the play with a dramatic

28-yard pass to receiver Freddie Mitchell, leading to a 20–17

Eagles victory that put Philadelphia in the NFC Championship

Game for the third year in a row. Despite having home-field

advantage, the Eagles lost to the Carolina Panthers 14–3,

missing the Super Bowl yet again.

In the off-season, Philadelphia made several high-

profile additions, including defensive end Hugh Douglas (a

fan favorite who returned to the club for a second stint),

Brian Dawkins made fewer interceptions than many NFL safeties; instead, his calling card was a punishing tackling style that often set the tempo for the Philadelphia defense. **X**

With his shifty moves and surprising power, halfback Brian Westbrook became one of the game's elite, all-purpose offensive weapons as a rusher, receiver, and kick returner. **X**

linebacker Jeremiah Trotter, and end Jevon Kearse, a pass-rushing specialist with such speed that he was nicknamed "The Freak." Offensively, the Eagles made a major splash by trading for Terrell Owens, a big, fast receiver who was known for both his exceptional talent and his often loudmouthed, showboating antics.

The reloaded Eagles flew high in 2004. McNabb and Owens connected for 14 touchdowns, Westbrook gained 1,515 total yards, and Philadelphia soared to a franchise-best 13–3 record. Even without Owens, who suffered a broken leg late in the season, the Eagles plowed through the Minnesota Vikings and Atlanta Falcons in the playoffs to reach the Super Bowl for the first time since 1980. They were up against the reigning champion New England Patriots in Super Bowl XXXIX, but the Eagles were confident that they would hold their own. The game was a close affair throughout, but the veteran

THE SANTA INCIDENT

Eagles fans are notoriously vocal and can sometimes be a bit out of control, as they displayed during halftime of a 1968 game when, in a famous incident, they pelted Santa Claus with snowballs. At the time, the Eagles franchise was becoming a perennial loser, in part because of moves made by team owner Jerry Wolman and coach and general manager Joe Kuharich. On December 15, when the Minnesota Vikings came to town, Eagles fans were supposed to be treated to a halftime Christmas pageant, complete with music and a decorated float. Due to a large snowfall, the pageant fell through, and the team instead hired 19-year-old Frank Olivo, a fan who had worn a Santa Claus costume to the game, to do an improvised run around the field. The disgruntled fans saw him as a representative of the team's poor management and used the plentiful snow to take out their frustrations on the poor volunteer with a shower of snowballs. Olivo escaped unharmed and without a grudge. He later said, "I'm a Philadelphia fan. I knew what was what. I thought it was funny."

A SUPER BOWL AT LAST

After three straight years of making it to the NFC Championship Game but coming up short, the Eagles finally earned their way into the big game after the 2004 season. Facing the reigning Super Bowl champion New England Patriots, the Eagles were the obvious underdogs in the matchup. The Eagles got a big boost before the game, though, when star receiver Terrell Owens—who was recovering from a fractured leg—was pronounced healthy enough to play. The Eagles struck first on Super Bowl Sunday when McNabb connected with tight end L. J. Smith (pictured) in the second quarter for a touchdown. At the end of three quarters, the game was knotted at 14–14. In the final quarter, the Patriots dominated the Eagles to jump ahead 24–14. Owens did his part, leading the team with 122 receiving yards, but the Eagles could not close the gap, losing 24–21. Although they lost, the Eagles had put up more of a fight than many experts predicted. "We just didn't make enough plays to get the victory," said Philadelphia cornerback Lito Sheppard, "and they didn't make that many mistakes."

Patriots were too much. New England celebrated a 24–21 win, while the Eagles went home empty-handed.

After a frustrating 2005 season in which the Eagles dropped to 6–10, Owens alienated his teammates and Philadelphia fans with a contract holdout, and McNabb was hampered by injuries, the team rebounded in 2006 to make the playoffs once again. When McNabb was sidelined by injury again late in the season, new backup quarterback Jeff Garcia stepped in and led the Eagles to five straight wins. After beating the Giants in a nail-biter in the first round of the playoffs, the Eagles fell to the New Orleans Saints, 27–24.

Although 2007 ended with the Eagles at the bottom of a tough NFC East with an 8–8 record, there were bright spots in which the Philadelphia faithful could find hope. Newly acquired wide receiver Kevin Curtis posted 1,110 yards, Westbrook remained a double-threat, and young defensive end Trent Cole solidified his status as one of the premier pass rushers in the NFL with 12.5 sacks.

Before the start of the 2008 season, the Eagles signed one of the league's top cornerbacks, Asante Samuel, and added defensive end Chris Clemons as one more threat to opposing quarterbacks. These players helped Philadelphia bounce back impressively in 2008. Although the Eagles went

X By early 2009, having played 10 pro seasons, quarterback Donovan McNabb had led Philadelphia to a 9–6 record over 15 playoff games.

RANDALL CUNNINGHAM

QUARTERBACK
EAGLES SEASONS: 1985-95
HEIGHT: 6-FOOT-4
WEIGHT: 212 POUNDS

What does a defense do when the opposing quarterback isn't just a pocket passer, or a traditional scrambler, but a real threat to run the ball for a touchdown from any distance? That's what defensive coordinators had to figure out when they faced the Eagles and Randall Cunningham. A superb all-around athlete, Cunningham had a strong arm, great speed, and the elusive moves of a star running back. After replacing Ron Jaworski as the starting quarterback in 1987, he gave Eagles fans a show they'd never forget. For the next four seasons, Cunningham was not only a prolific passer but the leading rusher on the team as well. In one 1989 game, he displayed yet another aspect of his athleticism with a surprise 91-yard punt that helped the Eagles beat the New York Giants in a key game. While the NFL has seen great passers, marvelous scramblers, and even some great runners at the quarterback position, perhaps no one put them together as well as Cunningham. His style of play paved the way for future fleet-footed quarterbacks such as Donovan McNabb to be more than just pocket passers.

[46]

a mere 9–6–1, they managed to sneak into the playoffs. Then the team started rolling, beating the Vikings and Giants on the road to advance to its fifth NFC Championship Game in eight years. Philadelphia looked bound for the Super Bowl when it led Arizona 25–24 in the fourth quarter, but the Cardinals mounted a final touchdown drive to end the Eagles' run one victory shy of the big game.

To many sports fans, the Philadelphia Eagles have come to represent the best of American football. From the helmetless Bill Hewitt and Chuck "60-Minute Man" Bednarik, to "The Minister of Defense" and the hard-nosed Donovan McNabb, Philadelphia players have always been tough. With today's Eagles eager to add to this seven-decade legacy of toughness in Philadelphia's new Lincoln Financial Field, there's no telling how high they might fly.

INDEX